SPIDERS

This edition published in 2007 by Voyageur Press, an imprint of MBI Publishing Company, Galtier Plaza, Suite 200, 380 Jackson Street, St. Paul, MN 55101-3885 USA

MBI Publishing Company titles are also available at discounts in bulk quantity for industrial or sales-promotional use. For details write to Special Sales Manager at MBI Publishing Company, Galtier Plaza, Suite 200, 380 Jackson Street, St. Paul, MN 55101-3885 USA.

ISBN 978-0-7603-3001-2

Photography copyright © 2007 by:

Front cover © Duncan Usher/ardea.com
Back cover © D Robert Franz/Franzfoto
Page 1 © Ingo Arndt/naturepl.com
Page 4 © NHPA/Hellio & Van Ingen
Page 6 © Bill Johnson
Page 9 © Ingo Arndt/naturepl.com
Page 10 © Bernard Castelein/naturepl.com
Page 13 © Ingo Arndt/naturepl.com
Page 15 © Ken Preston-Mafham/Premaphotos Wildlife
Page 16 © Simon Colmer/naturepl.com
Page 18 © Ingo Arndt/naturepl.com
Page 19 © Wegner/ARCO/naturepl.com
Page 20 © Phillippe Clement/naturepl.com
Page 23 © NHPA/Stephen Dalton
Page 24 © Ingo Arndt/naturepl.com
Page 25 © Ingo Arndt/naturepl.com
Page 26 © NHPA/Stephen Dalton
Page 29 © Ingo Arndt/naturepl.com
Page 30 © NHPA/Jany Sauvanet
Page 33 © Ken Preston-Mafham/Premaphotos Wildlife
Page 34 © NHPA/James Carmichael Jr

Page 38 © Ken Preston-Mafham/Premaphotos Wildlife
Page 39 © Rod Williams/naturepl.com
Page 40 © NHPA/Stephen Dalton
Page 43 © Lynn M Stone/naturepl.com
Page 44 © Ken Preston-Mafham/Premaphotos Wildlife
Page 47 © NHPA/Stephen Dalton
Page 48 © Ken Preston-Mafham/Premaphotos Wildlife
Page 49 © NHPA/Robert Erwin
Page 50 © Kim Taylor/naturepl.com
Page 53 © NHPA/James Carmichael Jr
Page 54 © NHPA/Stephen Dalton
Page 57 © Nick Garbutt/naturepl.com
Page 58 © Georgette Douwma/naturepl.com
Page 60 © Nick Garbutt/naturepl.com
Page 61 © Niall Benvie/naturepl.com
Page 62 © Ken Preston-Mafham/Premaphotos Wildlife
Page 65 © Ken Preston-Mafham/Premaphotos Wildlife
Page 66 © NHPA/James Carmichael Jr
page 69 © Ken Preston-Mafham/Premaphotos Wildlife
Page 72 © Laurie Campbell

Printed in China

Front Cover Photo: Wolf spider.   *Back cover photo*: Alpine spider.
Page 1: Jumping spider.   *Page 45*: A female decoy spider on a stabilimentum.

SPIDERS

Rod Preston-Mafham

Voyageur Press

Contents

What is a Spider?

Everyone can recognize a spider when they see one, or at least they can distinguish them from an insect. Insects usually have wings and three pairs of legs, while the spider has four pairs of legs and no wings. Although there is considerable variation in overall shape, all spiders are built to the same basic design. The body is divided into two sections, the cephalothorax and the abdomen, joined together by a narrow waist or pedicel. The cephalothorax consists of the head at the front joined directly onto the thorax, unlike insects where they are two separate entities. The exoskeleton of the cephalothorax is fairly tough in comparison to that of the abdomen, which is soft and easily damaged.

On the spider's head are a number of different structures. There may be two, six or eight eyes, their numbers and layout help in the classification of the various families. There is a pair of jaws, or chelicerae, which consist of a basal section onto which hinges a sharp fang, used to pierce prey and inject venom into it. Associated with the jaws, which hold the prey, is a pair of smaller structures used for chewing it once it has been caught. On either side of the jaws is what looks like a small leg. This is the pedipalp, (usually abbreviated to palp), associated with the sense of taste. In male spiders, however, the last segment of the palp is used during the mating process and may have a very complicated structure.

The upper surface of the spider's thorax is covered by a strong plate called the carapace. Attached to the thorax are the four pairs of walking legs, which are very similar in structure to those of an insect. Apart, however, from differences in length and thickness there are none of the modifications for digging or swimming that are found in a number of insect groups.

The spider abdomen usually has no visible structures on the upper surface, the exceptions being a number of species with peculiar horns or spines of varying shapes and lengths. From front to back on the underside, however, a number of features may be

A male grass spider. The spoon-shaped structures are the tips of the palps.

7

distinguished. In many spiders a pair of circular marks may be seen, which show the presence of the book lungs (used for obtaining oxygen from the air), by their openings to the outside. Just behind these, in the midline and in females only, is a structure called the epigyne, which is involved in the spiders' rather unusual mating technique. In both males and females there then comes a furrow running across the abdomen, into which open the reproductive organs of each sex. At the hind end of the abdomen is the opening of the anus, around or in front of which are the silk-producing spinnerets. Just ahead of the spinnerets is the centrally placed tracheal spiracle, which opens into a different kind of gas exchange system separate from the book lungs.

Inside Spiders

Internally, like most animals, spiders have a gut, a blood system with a heart, a system like the kidneys for getting rid of waste, gas exchange structures for obtaining oxygen and male or female reproductive organs.

The gut runs from mouth to anus. At the front end there is a sucking stomach that the spider uses to take in its predigested food. Once they have subdued their prey spiders feed in one of two different ways. They may inject digestive enzymes into the prey through holes cut with the fangs, and then suck up the liquid so produced, or they chew the prey up, pouring enzymes onto it as they do so and sucking up the resultant liquid remains. The outcome of the first method is an empty husk of the original prey, that of the second an unrecognizable ball of chewed up remains. Any solid bits and pieces are filtered out by bristles in the mouth and throat and the liquid food then passes into the rest of the gut where final digestion, and absorption, of the food takes place.

The abdomen of the spider is rather delicate and unless they can subdue their prey very rapidly they could easily be injured. It is to this end that all spiders, with the exception of a single family, inject their struggling prey with poison. The poison is produced in special

This spider, the Mexican beauty Brachypelma boehmi, *is more likely to be seen in a pet shop than in the wild as it easily breeds in captivity. Its hairiness is typical of the family Theraphosidae, which includes the bird-eating spiders.*

A golden orb or giant wood spider (Nephila maculata) *in her large
web of yellow silk. Such webs are strong enough to occasionally trap small birds
or even bats, which the spider is quite prepared to eat.*

glands and passes down a narrow tube and out through a small opening near the tip of the fang. While the glands are small and restricted to the head in the tarantulas and their relations (the Mygalamorphae), in the true spiders (the Araneomorphae), the glands are larger and in some may extend well back into the cephalothorax. In the majority of spiders the poison contains mainly neurotoxins, which rapidly disable the prey's nervous system, so that any struggle is reduced to a minimum.

Spiders have the usual arthropod open circulatory system where blood (haemolymph) is pumped from the heart and flows through the body cavity and around the main organs, rather than through discrete vessels. Blood is also directed down one side of each of the appendages and back up the other to supply the muscles they contain. Spider blood contains the oxygen-transporting pigment haemocyanin. In spiders with book lungs the blood passes through these and oxygen is picked up by the haemocyanin to be carried to the rest of the body. Book lungs are, in fact, the more primitive of the two types of gas exchange structures to be found in spiders. They are best described as having air spaces interleaved with blood spaces, like alternative pages in a book, with little pillars holding the 'pages' apart. The mygalomorph spiders have only this system. True spiders may have both book lungs and a tracheal system resembling that of insects. The tracheal system consists of a system of strengthened tubes, the largest open to the outside through the tracheal spiracle. These branch and get smaller and smaller until they permeate the various organs, to which oxygen is delivered by diffusion. This system is more efficient than the book lung and means that those spiders with it can be more active than the slow-moving mygalomorphs.

The reproductive organs have the same basic design as that of most animals. Male spiders have a pair of testes, which form a common duct opening to the outside of the abdomen. Females have a pair of ovaries, which unite in a common oviduct, which then forms a uterus before again opening to the outside. In the majority of adult female spiders this opening is covered by a special plate, the epigyne. In addition, the females have a pair of sacs, the spermothecae, into which sperm is injected during mating and is stored until the eggs require to be fertilized during egg-laying.

Although basically the same in design as that of other arthropods the central nervous system is somewhat condensed. Most of it, including a simple brain, is in the cephalothorax from which nerves run to and from the legs and to the abdominal organs.

Spider Senses

The most obvious spider sense organs are the eyes. Some spiders have just two eyes, while others have six or eight depending upon the family they belong to. Web-dwelling spiders tend on the whole to have small eyes, which probably have a limited ability to form images but are very sensitive to changes in light intensity, i.e., night and day, or to shadows falling over them. The hunters have larger eyes, especially the center pair of the front row, and these are able to form images. These large eyes are most obvious in the jumping spiders, which actively hunt their prey during the hours of daylight. Shine a flashlight onto the ground in a North American forest at night and you are likely to see many pairs of what look like tiny headlights shining back at you. These are the main eyes of wolf spiders, which are usually sit-and-wait hunters who can be active both at night and during the day.

The large, median pair of eyes of the hunters are the most specialized, for not only can they form an image but the also have the ability to focus. This process is different than that of humans for instead of the lens focussing and the retina remaining stationary, in spiders the lens is fixed and it is the retina that moves in relation to it. Take a close look at a jumping spider's anterior median eyes and you will detect a slight flickering movement in them as the retina moves during focussing.

Spiders in general are rather hairy creatures and this relates to their well-developed tactile senses. The majority of spiders are nocturnal so that touch and feel are more

The wolf spiders are sit-and-wait hunters, with large, forward-facing main eyes which are used to detect passing prey items. The sharp fangs used to pierce and hold the prey are clearly visible.

important than sight. It has been found experimentally that touching a single hair of a resting spider will bring about some form of immediate response. With numerous hairs in contact with the substrate on which it is sitting, or in contact with its web, the spider is able to appreciate the vibrations produced by approaching prey items, or enemies, and can make the appropriate response. Spiders have no ears as such but they do have special hairs called trichobothria, which are sensitive to low frequency sounds such as those made by the wings of an insect, or by the movement of a spider of the opposite sex. These special hairs are referred to as 'touch at a distance' receptors. They are found on the legs and actually allow the spider to orientate to the direction of the incoming signal.

Unpalatable prey items caught in a spider web are usually cut out and released. This indicates that spiders have a sense of taste. Watch a spider approaching prey in its web and you will see that the first thing it does, before biting it, is to touch it with the front legs or the palps, both of which contain taste receptors. Even after it has accepted a prey item a spider may then discard it, indicating that it has a further sense of taste in the mouth region.

Relatives of the Spiders

Not all eight-legged creatures are spiders, but the rest are close relatives. These include scorpions and tailed whip-scorpions, which are easy to recognize, for they have an elongated abdomen with a sting or whip on the end and the palps are large and adapted for grabbing prey. Tailless whip-scorpions are a bit more spider-like but they have a flattened body, large grasping pedipalps and the front pair of legs are extremely long. It is the harvestmen and the mites and ticks, which are the most difficult for the beginner to distinguish from spiders. In spiders the cephalothorax is separated from the abdomen by a distinct waist but in the other two groups the head, thorax and abdomen are joined together as a single unit.

A female sheetweb spider feeds on a parent bug, despite the bug's offensive smell.

The Variety of Spiders

Somewhere in excess of 34,000 species of spider have so far been described from over 100 families. Like all living organisms each species of spider has its own scientific name, usually written in italics in text. In each scientific name the genus comes first and starts with a capital letter while the species name comes second. *Misumena vatia* is, for example, common over most of North America and as such also has a common name, the flower spider or goldenrod spider. Unfortunately, relatively few species have common names and in discussing the characteristics of the spider families it will often be necessary to use the scientific name alone.

There are two major groups of spiders. Relatively primitive are the Mygalomorphae, the tarantulas and their relatives. The majority of spiders met by the average person are the modern, or 'true' spiders, the Araneomorphae. The mygalomorphs include many of the world's largest species. In fact the largest known spider in the world is the so-called Goliath spider, *Theraphosa leblondi*, with a body length exceeding 4in (10cm) and a leg-span in males up to 12in (30cm). Females can be more than 4oz (110g) in weight and their fangs can be up to one inch (25mm) long. In contrast to these giants the group also contains tiny species less than 0.035in (1mm) long but it is the true spiders that contain the smallest known spiders, all in the family Symphytognathidae. Quite which is the smallest is not yet clear since both sexes are not yet known for some of these tiny spiders. *Patu marplesi* from Samoa, for example, has males of body length 0.017in (0.4mm), with males of *P. digua* from Columbia a fraction smaller than this. What is likely to be the smallest of all is the male of *Anapistula caecula* from the Ivory Coast. The females are just 0.02in (0.46mm) long and the males are likely to be between one half and one third this length, making them almost invisible to the naked eye.

The normally white goldenrod spider occasionally turns yellow for a day or so.

Distinguishing a mygalomorph from a true spider externally is fairly simple, for the jaws are arranged differently in each group. Mygalomorphs have jaws that run parallel to the line of the body and strike downwards into their prey. This works fine for these spiders, which live mostly on the ground or on trees, so that they have something to bite against. On something like a leaf, however, a downward strike would probably fail to pierce the prey as the leaf would bend away against the pressure. This problem has been overcome by the true spiders, for their jaws bite against one another, from side to side, in a pincerlike action.

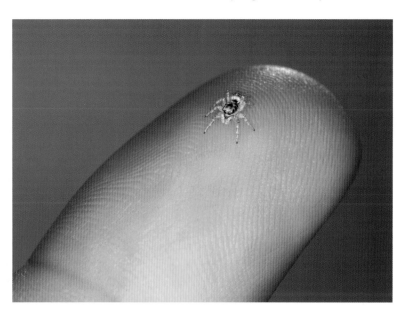

A zebra spider, Salticus scenicus.

The Mygalomorphae
(Tarantulas and their Relatives)

There are four major families within the tarantula group, probably the best known of which are the the so-called 'bird-eating spiders'. Although a number of them live in trees and occasionally catch birds, many of them live in uncapped burrows, from which they emerge to catch passing prey. Some species are popular as pets and overcollecting has reduced their populations to dangerously low levels in the wild. Some do however readily breed in captivity. Trapdoor spiders live in burrows in the ground, which they dig with the aid of a set of teeth on the basal segments of the jaws. Most place a lid over the burrow and sit beneath this waiting to leap out onto passing prey items. Another family contains the infamous Sydney funnelweb spider and its relations, whose poison is highly toxic to humans. As their name implies they build a sheet web with a funnel lair and

The mygalomorphs include all of the world's largest spiders.
Just how big they can get is illustrated by this San Sebastian pink bird-eating
spider, Pamphobeteus platyomma *sitting on a hand.*

rush out to grab any prey which walks on to the sheet. Some do live in burrows but in soft ground since they do not have the special teeth to aid in their digging. The purseweb spiders extend the silk lining of their burrows above the surface of the ground, either vertically or horizontally according to the species. Any prey walking over the purse is bitten through the purse wall. All four of these families have representatives in North America, while in Europe just trapdoor and purseweb spiders are found.

One single family shares features with both the mygalomorphs and the true spiders. They construct a lampshade-shaped web giving them their common name of lampshade weavers. At least 4 species of these spiders may be found in mountainous areas of North America. They resemble mygalomorphs in having book lungs, a similar heart and small poison glands but on the other hand they have a cribellum (see below), as in a number of true spider families. The jaw arrangement is intermediate between the two groups, though it is closer to that of the mygalomorphs.

The Araneomorphae (True Spiders)

Of the 90 true spider families only around one quarter of them are commonly seen and merit description. Two main sub-groups are recognised, one with simple reproductive organs and the other with more complex ones.

Spiders Families with Simple Reproductive Organs (Haplogyne):

This group contains a number of families with just six eyes. The family Oonopidae, or dwarf sixeyed spiders, are tiny, seldom exceeding 0.07in (2mm) in length. *Orchestina saltitans* may be seen hunting over walls and cupboards in human habitations from New England to Georgia and across as far as Missouri, while the similar *Oonops domesticus* occurs in similar situations in Europe. Two other families have members likely to be seen in homes on both

Banana or golden silk spider on her web in Central America.

sides of the Atlantic. The daddylonglegs or cellar spiders live in untidy webs in the corners of rooms and sheds. They have very long legs and either tubular or spherical abdomens. *Pholcus phalangioides* is cosmopolitan where temperatures do not fall below 50°F (10°C) and is common in the author's home where it often takes the fierce and much larger house spiders as prey. The six-eyed spiders of the family Segestriidae, or tunnel spiders, live in silken tubes built into suitable cracks in trees, rocks and on houses. From these radiate a number of triplines. When a prey item trips over one of these the spider rushes out and immobilizes it before dragging it into the tube to be consumed.

Perhaps the strangest of this group of families is the spitting spiders, with seven species from North America. The cephalothorax is domed, giving them the appearance of hunchbacks, for the thorax contains the enlarged poison glands. These produce not only poison but also a sticky liquid. The spider moves its head from side to side as it spits out sticky strands, which are spread over the prey, anchoring it to the substrate. The head movement is so rapid that it cannot be discerned by the human eye.

Spiders with Complex Reproductive Organs (Entelegynae):

Within this group a minority of families possess a cribellum, represented by just three species in both North America and Europe. The family Uloboridae, the hackled orbweaver spiders produce orb webs, or sectors of orb webs, and are unique in that they do not have poison glands and just wrap prey to immobilize it. The family Dictynidae, the meshweaver spiders, is well represented by the genus *Dictyna*. They are small spiders, with a rather globular abdomen, seldom exceeding 3/16in (5mm) in body length. They make rather untidy webs on vegetation, walls or rock faces. The Amaurobiidae, the hackledmesh, or lace weavers, are larger and more elongate and they usually make their equally untidy webs on the ground or in cracks in walls or under rocks.

The famous spitting spider, Scytodes thoracica *with its enlarged cephalothorax.*

The remaining families lack a cribellum and those considered here contain species most likely to be encountered on a day to day basis. Perhaps the most commonly met with spiders are the orbweavers, of which there are two main families, the Tetragnathidae and the Araneidae. The Tetragnathidae, the longjawed orbweavers, are so-called on account of their elongated jaws. These bear projections in both sexes, which enable them to lock together during mating, presumably to reduce the likelihood that the female will attack the male or vice-versa. Members of the genus *Tetragnatha* are elongate spiders, often found near water, with an orb web, which is placed near the horizontal rather than upright. Also now included in this family are the *Nephila* species. *N. clavipes*, the golden-silk spider is a tropical species, which is also found in the southeastern USA. The females are large, with the

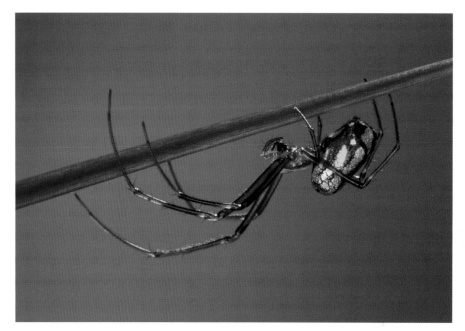

The orchard orbweaver lives in low vegetation in eastern USA.

body usually exceeding one inch (25mm) in length, and they live in a large orb web made of yellowish colored silk. The males are just one quarter the size of the females, while in other *Nephila* species males account for just one hundredth of the weight of the female.

The most typical orbweavers are in the family Araneidae, with more than 150 species from North America, and because their webs are so visible they themselves are perhaps

One of the world's most colorful species, the ladybird spider, comes from Europe.

the most noticed of all spiders. A typical family member has a rather rounded abodmen and either sits at the center of its web or in a lair close to it. Running from the web to the lair is a signal line, which the spider holds by one leg and which tells it if prey has become trapped. The spider can then rush, usually downwards from the lair, to bite and wrap its captive. A number of tropical species have a more flattened abdomen with bizarre extensions in the form of spikes or horns, whose exact function is not clear. A few members have given up webs altogether and live more like crab spiders.

The cobweb weaver spiders build webs like untidy scaffolding, either in vegetation or close to the ground. They have even more globular abdomens than the araneids and are usually rather shiny spiders. The widow spiders are members of this family. The sheetweb spiders are a large family that build sheet webs in the form of a hammock. Their abdomens are rather more elongate than those of the two previous families. The sub-family Erigoninae contains many tiny species, a fraction of an inch (a few millimetres) long, which are often found in tens of thousands in grassland. Spiders of this family are easily recognized for they hang below their hammock web waiting for prey to fall on to it. Last but not least amongst the web-builders are the funnel weaver spiders. This family includes the house spider, *Tegenaria domestica*, a cosmopolitan species, and other members of the genus imported into North America but native to Europe. Those which live in the proximity of man build their sheet webs, narrowing down to a funnel lair, in the corners of unused rooms, sheds and barns.

Spiders that no longer use webs take a bit more searching out than the web-builders but nevertheless many of them may be encountered on a regular basis. The crab spiders are sit-and-wait predators named from the fact that they do bear some resemblance to crabs in their overall shape and they also have a tendency to scuttle sideways like crabs. Most often encountered are the flower spiders, *Misumena vatia* from Europe, introduced

A female green crab spider in a pose typical of its family, waiting for prey to arrive.

into and now all over North America, and the similar native North American *Misumenops* species. These spiders have the interesting ability to change color from white to yellow and back again over a period of some hours. Since one is as likely to find a blue or pink flower with either form on it, quite what the value of this change is we are not certain. Combining dashing from one place to another with periods of sit-and-wait for passing prey is the habit of many of the wolf spiders. These include the numerous *Pardosa* species, usually brown to black in color, which may be found running over the ground or low vegetation all over North America and Europe. They are at their most noticeable when the females are carrying their pale-colored egg-sacs attached to the end of the abdomen. Much larger are the *Lycosa* species, which include members that build lairs under stones or live in silk-lined burrows, as well as being free-living. *Lycosa carolinensis*, a widespread North American species, is quite a large spider, though it will have to be searched for on the ground with a flashlight, for it is mainly nocturnal. The female body length can reach nearly 1½in (35mm), so it is quite impressive. Resembling the mainly ground-dwelling wolf spiders, and sometimes given their common name, are the nursery web or fisher spiders. They are, however, more likely to be found living amongst vegetation or, in the case of the fisher spiders, hunting on the surface of lakes and ponds.

Perhaps the most endearing of spiders are the jumping spiders of the family Salticidae, the largest of the spider families with more than 4000 species described worldwide. Their main characteristic is their very large pair of forward-facing eyes, with which they find their prey as they hunt actively through vegetation, on rocks and walls or on the ground. They occur in their greatest numbers in tropical regions, where many are brightly colored, resembling living jewels. There are more than 200 species in North America, with more and more brightly colored species in warmer, southern climes.

With their large eyes, the jumpers are perhaps the most endearing of all spiders.

The Life of Spiders

It is necessary to consider the unique way in which spiders mate before looking at how the male spider finds and courts his partner. In both sexes reproductive ducts open at the genital pore. The male spider has no abdominal structure with which to introduce seminal fluid, containing his sperm, into the female. Instead, he uses the specially modified terminal segments of his palps. In its simplest form, in more primitive spider families, the structure of the palp is akin to that of a simple bulb pipette but in higher spiders the palp can have a very complicated structure built around this simple basic form. In the families with complex sex organs the male of each species has his own unique palpal arrangement and this matches exactly the structure of the epigyne of the female of the same species. This sort of lock and key arrangement helps to prevent cross mating between different but closely related species. Once the palp is inserted into the female, muscles squeeze on the bulb and the semen passes out to be stored in the spermathecae.

With the exception of the gossamer, or sheetweb spiders, males have to charge their palps, a process called sperm induction, before they go in search of a mate. This involves filling the reservoir bulb of the palp with semen. One might expect this to be a simple action, the male sucking the semen up as he releases it from his reproductive opening; in fact this never happens. Instead the male constructs a special sperm web onto which a drop of semen is placed before it is sucked up into the palp. The sperm web varies from being a single line of silk held between the front legs, as in daddylongleg males, to an extensive sheet web in mygalomorph males. More typically a miniature web is constructed, males of the garden spider *Araneus diadematus* illustrating a typical example. He spins a tiny, rectangular web and exudes a drop of semen onto the upper surface. Most males then chew their palps for a while, seemingly to make it easier to take the semen up. The male garden spider then dips his

Not a fight, but the rather intimidating courtship of a pair of goliath bird-eating spiders.

palp into the drop of semen and sucks it up. The process of sperm induction typically takes from 10 to 15 minutes, though it takes much longer in mygalomorphs. Having charged his palps, the male can now go in search of a receptive female.

Finding a Mate

With the exception of the few social species, spiders are very much loners, so how do they manage to find one another when the time comes to produce the next generation? Like the insects, female spiders rely upon the production of pheromones, chemical messengers, in order to indicate their presence to males of the same species. How the pheromones are employed depends upon the type of spider but in all cases the males detect them by means of their tarsal organs, situated on their front legs. As they move around their environment, female spiders that do not build webs leave a silk dragline behind them, which they impregnate with pheromones. All the male has to do, therefore, is to find one of these and follow it until he finds her at the end, a ploy typical of wolf spiders. Female fishing spiders, on the other hand, release pheromones onto the surface of the water on which they hunt.

Following silken lines to find a mate seems quite straightforward but how do you find her when she lives in a web, which may be suspended many feet above the ground? Orbweaver males, for example, are often tiny compared with the females, yet several of them find their way to a female's web. The answer to this is that the females release airborne pheromones to attract the males towards them. This is obviously more efficient than crawling around the vegetation in the hope of stumbling across a female in her web.

Courtship and Mating

Having found a female the male now has to indicate that he is of the right caliber to father her offspring. This involves a period of courtship, which can vary from very short to quite prolonged and complicated. The reason for at least some form of courtship becomes

*The male garden spider on the left courts a larger female
in her web. If she is not interested in his advances she may jump at
him, whereupon he will drop to safety on his dragline.*

The green lynx spider is common over much of the
southern half of the USA. Here, the male on the left signals
to a slightly bulkier female during courtship.

obvious when considering that both male and female spiders are predators and that a wrong move could end up with one of them becoming a meal for the other. A further reason for courtship is that in some cases the female has to be induced to adopt a particular pose before mating can take place. The way in which courtship takes place relates in the main to the species' visual abilities. Thus in poor-sighted spiders courtship tends to be tactile, while in those with large, image-forming eyes courtship is much more visual.

There is, however, one other sense used in courtship, with examples known from more than twenty spiders families, and that is the use of sound and vibrations. This involves either stridulation, where one part of the body is rubbed against another to generate sound, or part of the body is tapped or drummed upon the substrate, most often a leaf. In Europe the male of the buzzing spider, *Anyphaena accentuata*, drums rapidly upon a leaf with his abdomen, the sound he produces being audible to humans. He usually does this on a leaf above the female's nest. She immediately rushes out and grapples with him before retiring back to her nest, followed by the male who is then presumably allowed to mate with her. While the buzzing spider lives in trees, several North American wolf spiders of the genus *Lycosa*, which are ground dwellers, are mainly active at night and also use sound courtship. *Lycosa gulosa* males, for example, drum on dead leaves on the forest floor producing a sound that can be heard up to 20ft (6m) away. *Lycosa rabida* males also use courtship sounds at night but during the day, when this species may also be active, females will mate without the use of acoustic signals.

Day-active, well-sighted spiders on the other hand, tend to rely upon visual signals during courtship. *Pardosa* species males from both Europe and North America wave their palps in front of the female in a pattern unique to each species. An interesting aside at this point, relating to the role of pheromones, is that a male will continue to signal to a position just vacated by a female, presumably because he can smell that she appears to be there, even if she is not. Male jumping spiders use not only their palps but also their legs and their whole body in often quite complex displays. As well as being brightly colored they may also have tufts of hairs and patches of scales which add to their overall attraction to the opposite sex.

Almost no courtship is found in some of the short-sighted nocturnal hunters, where maybe contact between a correct-smelling, ready-to-mate pair is all that is required. Courtship also seems to be lacking in the huge *Nephila* species spiders, where the females may be 100 times the weight of the male. Here, it would seem that the male is below the size at which he would be considered worth eating, so when she is receptive he can mate at his leisure. Most short-sighted web-dwellers do, however, have a degree of courtship which is tactile in nature and involves the male entering the female's web. He announces his presence by vibrating or plucking at the web with a predetermined set of signals, which the female understands. This compares with the random vibrations, which would be produced by a prey insect thrashing around trying to escape from the web. If the female is receptive, then she will allow the male to approach and mate with her. Males of *Meta segmentata* in Europe enhance their chances of success by courting the female while she is feeding. Whilst so engrossed he will tickle her with his long front legs and, if she responds to his advances he constructs a special thread of silk onto which she must be coaxed prior to mating. Males of this species may spend a few days in the female's web before courtship commences, and where a web contains more than one male, a fight to the death may take place between them. The loser may then end up as the titbit on which the female feeds while the victorious male courts and mates with her.

Much has been written about courtship in *Araneus diadematus*, the garden spider from Europe, now found over large areas of North America. Like the previous species the male has to get the female onto his nuptial thread before mating can take place. Although he is in some danger from the somewhat larger female, reports of high levels of cannibalism of the male by the female are, in the author's experience, considerably exaggerated. Each year in his garden in the UK there may be dozens of female garden spiders in their webs, with ardent males in many of them going about their business of seducing the females. During this time males may occasionally end up as a meal for the females but usually this is towards the end of the breeding season, when the males are going to die anyway. Although there is some cannibalism of males by females in a number of different species it would seem that in most instances this is the exception rather than the rule and indeed the female sometimes ends up as a meal for the male.

One way of keeping control of the female during mating is to tie her down with silk. Males of the crab spider *Xysticus cristatus* from Europe, having approached the female and gained consent to mate, tie her down to a leaf with a few strands of silk before actual mating takes place. It would appear that the silk only gives the female the impression that she is tied down, for following mating, she breaks from the silk with ease. Such a ploy is also found in the North American nursery web spider, *Pisaurina maura*. Here, however, following a short courtship the female jumps off a leaf and hangs motionless on a short thread of silk, her legs clasped to the side of her body. The male follows her down and, spinning her around, ties her up with strands of silk before mating with her. Once again, following copulation, the female easily breaks free of her bonds.

Finally comes a courtship ploy which, so far as is presently known, is unique to the spider *Pisaura mirabilis* from Europe. Before attempting to find a mate the male must first of all catch some suitable prey, which often as not is a fly. Normally, he would now consume it without any further action but in this instance he swathes it in silk until it resembles a shiny white ball. He now goes in search of a female, walking in a jerky, robotlike manner as he does so. Having found a receptive female he approaches her from the front, holding his 'gift' up ahead of him. She then moves slowly forwards and attempts to grab the gift in her jaws. Initially, the male leans back and prevents this but finally he lets her start feeding on it and takes his chance to begin mating. Copulation may take an hour or more, though every now and again the male may break off and join the female in having a meal from his gift.

Egg-Laying and Parental Care

There is a roughly positive relationship between the number of eggs laid in a batch and the size of the female. The smallest spiders, those less than 1/50in (0.5mm), lay but a single egg. Large spiders, such as female *Nephila* species, may lay more than a thousand eggs in a single batch and have been known to produce around 4500 in a lifetime. The bolas spider *Mastophora dizzydeani*, from Colombia, goes one better than this with a total lifetime

An ant-mimicking spider weaves her egg-sac.

output of more than 9000 eggs. In at least six spider families not all of the eggs are fertile, and the infertile ones are used as an initial source of food for the spiderlings when they hatch. Perhaps more gruesome are a couple of species of jumping spider, where the early hatchlings then cannibalize their later developing brothers and sisters.

Whatever her size the female spider spins at least some form of an egg-sac to contain her batch of eggs.

Perhaps the simplest egg-sac is that of the Pholcidae, consisting of just enough strands of silk to hold the eggs together, and the loosely packed bundle is held in the female's jaws until they hatch. More usually the eggs, which are covered in sticky mucus, adhere to a silk pad and to one another, and the whole batch is then covered in further layers of silk. Coincidentally, the eggs are fertilized, as they are laid, with the sperm that was stored in the

A female black widow spider hangs in her untidy web next to her egg-sac.

spermathecae during mating. The silk on some egg-sacs changes color with time so that it blends into the background on which it was laid. Some spiders, e.g., female two-tailed spiders, cover the egg-sac with flakes of bark and lichen, while other species utilize bits off prey items, which form a perfect camouflage.

The fate of the egg-sacs varies very much from family to family. They may be completely abandoned by the female, though normally they are well-hidden. Alternatively the female may stand guard over them until they hatch, before abandoning the young. In some instances, this just involves the female sitting in the open, or hidden beneath a stone or other object, next to her eggs. Some females, however, go to the trouble of making a distinct nest in which to hide them. Interesting examples of nest-building include *Pellenes nigrociliatus*, who makes her nest in empty snail shells, which are then suspended in vegetation by silken lines, out of harm's way. A *Euryattus* species from Australia suspends a rolled up leaf about 3ft (1m) above the ground, supporting it there by a number of scaffold lines. She then places as many as seven egg sacs into her aerial hideaway. The European grass spider, *Agelena labyrinthica*, weaves a silk labyrinth in the center of which she places her egg-sac. This may act to deter parasitic wasps, who are unable to find their way to the eggs through the complexity of the labyrinth. *Pisaurina mira* from North America and *Pisaura mirabilis* from Europe carry their egg-sacs around in their jaws as a means of protecting them. When the young are close to hatching, they then construct silken nursery tents in which they place their egg-sac, and stand guard over them until the babies hatch and disperse. Wolf spiders also carry their egg-sacs around but attached to their spinnerets. This gives them a distinct advantage over the pisaurids, for their jaws are still free to kill prey.

Guarding of the egg-sac is a form of parental care but this behavior is carried even

These newly-hatched spiders will stay together for a few days before dispersing.

41

further by some spiders. In a number of species the young remain in the web and the female shares food with them. The most advanced form of parental care, however, is found in the so-called mothercare spiders, of which the European species, *Theridion sisyphium*, a denizen of the author's garden, is perhaps the most documented. In low bushes the female builds her scaffold web in which she incorporates a tent-like lair, usually festooned with the remains of prey and other detritus. She keeps her egg-sac in her lair until her babies hatch, feeding on whatever is trapped in her web, but does not at first share this with her offspring. Instead, at intervals, they rush over to her and shake her by the legs, an indication to her that they are hungry. If she is receptive to their advances a liquid, sometimes referred to as 'spider milk', oozes from her mouth and the babies commences to suck it up. This 'milk' is very rich in nutrients as it is predigested prey plus cells from the lining of the mother's intestine. As a result of this care the young grow very fast and it is not long before they are big enough to share in their mother's prey.

In at least three spider families the final act the female makes is to provide her worn out body for the young to feed on. This may just be a case of the female dying as a result of her toils and the young feeding on her decomposing corpse. In the case of some *Stegodyphus* species females, from the family Eresidae, the situation is taken one stage further. As she reaches old age and with a growing brood of offspring, internal enzyme digestion turns her into a liquid broth, on which they feed when she eventually dies.

Like insects, spiders grow by passing through a series of molts before they reach adulthood. The newly hatched spiderling molts once before if commences catching prey and feeding. It then feeds and grows to the limit of its present skin before its molts, stretching the new skin to its full size before it hardens. Once the araneomorph spiders mature, they never molt again. The mygalomorphs are, however, much longer lived, some females achieving 30 or more years. They therefore molt at intervals over their long life, to repair the inevitable damage to their external sensory hairs and other structures.

The long-lived mygalomorph spiders molt at intervals
after they become mature. On the right a female whiteknee
tarantula stands next to her old skin.

Silk and its Uses

It seems likely that the earliest role of silk in the life of the spider is for the lining of the burrow in which they dwell. Silk maintains the integrity of the burrow wall and provides an even surface on which the spider can climb up to catch passing prey. As time passes so silk is used for other purposes, notably to form the structure of the prey-catching web, and also to form the egg-sac to protect the eggs and prevent them from drying out.

Spider silk is related to keratin, the basic structural protein of hair and feathers in vertebrates and silk in insects. It is, however, much stronger than insect silk and differs in structure and adaptability. Most of what is known about the structure of spider silk comes from research on the dragline of *Nephila* orbweavers. The protein in this silk is called fibroin and itself combines the proteins spidroin 1 and spidroin 2, their exact composition varying from species to species and on the spider's diet. The main amino acids in fibroin are alanine, roughly 25%, and glycine, around 42%. The presence of these two amino acids is highly significant for they are small molecules, without any side chains, and are ideal for the formation of larger molecules, where stretching and sliding past one another is important.

The actual structure of silk protein is very complex but essentially it consists of alternate rigid and elastic sections arranged in a helix. The rigid sections are made up of alanine molecules whereas the elastic regions are made up of repeating groups of glycine molecules. The elasticity of the silk appears to depend upon the number of these glycine groups between each of the rigid alanine groups. Capture silk, for example, has 43 glycine groups and can extend to more than 200% of its original length, while dragline silk has only about nine units and can stretch to just 30% of its original length. When at rest the protein in the silk is in disarray. When the silk is stretched the proteins are pulled into a neater configuration, an act which they resist. As tension on the silk is released, the proteins contract to their original state. This is most important in catching threads, for this property of silk allows it to absorb the energy of an insect crashing into the web, without the silk breaking.

Although silk is a protein it does not decompose like most proteins, evidenced by cobwebs many years old in the corners of long disused buildings. This is because the silk thread has an outer membrane containing certain chemicals important in maintaining its longevity. The first of these is the substance pyrolodin, which binds tightly to water molecules and therefore helps prevent the threads from drying out. Two salts are also present. Potassium hydrogen phosphate maintains a level of acidity on the thread, which inhibits the growth of bacteria and fungi and this is reinforced by the presence of potassium nitrate.

Silk is formed in a series of glands in the spider abdomen, these glands opening to the exterior through little nozzles, the spigots, on the spinnerets. Six different types of gland are recognized in spiders, though not every species possesses every kind of gland. A common spider, which does have the lot, is the garden spider, *Araneus diadematus*. The glands and the function of the silk that they produce are as follows: **Aciniform glands**: silk for wrapping prey and also the soft silk for the inner lining of the egg-sac. **Cylindrical or tubuliforme glands**: not in male spiders and used to make the tough silk that covers the egg-sac. **Ampullate glands**: dragline silk and structural silk. Occur as major and minor glands. **Pyriform glands**: produce the silk for the anchoring of structural lines to the substrate. **Aggregate glands**: these produce the sticky globules, which are attached to the web trapping lines. **Flagelliform glands**: responsible for the spirals of silk onto which the sticky globules are placed.

The silk reaches the end of the spigots in a liquid form but as it is pulled out by the spider so it hardens and achieves its final form. The way in which the spider pulls on the silk can affect its properties in that the harder it pulls the stronger it becomes. The spigots also have some control over the diameter of the threads that are produced. In terms of size, *Nephila* dragline silk has a diameter of around 0.00032in (0.008mm), garden spider (Araneus diadematus) silk is typically 0.00012 (0.003mm) in diameter while the finest silks are just 0.0000008in (0.00002mm) across.

Triangle spiders weave just a small section of an orb web and attach the broad end
to neighbouring vegetation. They then, as shown here, hold on to the narrow end, and when
something flies into the web, they let it loose to wrap around and capture the prey.

The cribellate spiders have an extra gland, in front of the spinnerets, called the cribellum. This appears as a flat plate, which can have anything from 100 to 50000 spigots on it. These produce very fine silk, strengthened with lesser numbers of larger fibres, which are fluffed out by a special comb, the calamistrum, on each hind leg to produce the non-sticky, hackled-band lines of this group of spiders.

Silk is also used by spiders in a rather less obvious but very important role, that of distribution from their place of birth, a necessity to prevent overcrowding. Unlike insects, which have wings, spiders fly in a different way, by ballooning. This phenomenon is only possible in immature spiders or those who are tiny as adults, mainly the small linyphiids. On warm, fall days with a light wind countless millions of spiders take to the air, simply by standing on tiptoe at some high point and releasing a line of silk into the breeze. This is picked up by

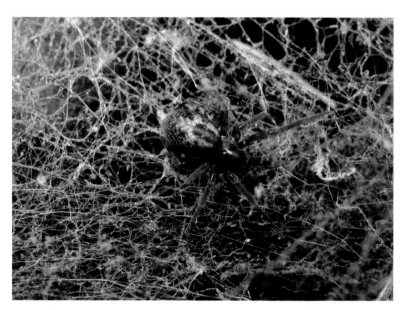

A lace-weaver on her web of hackled-band silk.

the wind, and when it reaches the right length the spider lets go and drifts off to who knows where. They have little or no control on where they go and a very large percentage of them will perish, ending up in some totally unsuitable environment. The distances traveled by these aeronauts can be huge, for they have been found thousands of feet up in the air in the aerial plankton at the mercy of the prevailing winds.

Newly-hatched babies of the black widow spider in their mother's web.

Catching Prey

All spiders are predators and the way in which they catch their prey falls basically into two categories. They either use a web, in its broadest sense, or they do not. Broadest sense is relevant here for, as we shall see, some spiders have reduced their web to a single trapline.

The Mygalomorphae (Tarantulas and their Relatives)

Taking first the mygalomorph spiders, they fall into two main groups. The majority of them are sit-and-wait predators, remaining in their silk-lined burrows in the soil and leaping out on passing prey as they detect the vibrations produced as it walks past. Since they will eat almost anything they are sure to catch something every now and again. The radius of detection of the prey may be increased in some species by having silk triplines radiating out from the mouth of the burrow. Any insect walking over and touching one of these will bring an immediate reaction from the spider. The Australian spider *Agannipe raphiduca* uses radiating twigs as triplines, each connected to the mouth of the burrow by a short length of silk. Presumably tripping over a twig produces a greater stimulus than simply tripping over a line of silk. The purseweb spiders also live in silk-lined burrows but this is extended as a closed tube so that it lies either across the ground or up the surrounding vegetation. The spider lies in this extension and if a prey item walks over it, the spider plunges its fangs into it through the silk walls. It then uses a set of saw-like teeth on the basal segment of the jaw to cut through the silk, so that it can pull the prey into the purse, from where it is taken into the burrow to be consumed.

The theraphosids, which includes the bird-eating spiders, are free-living. They are mainly nocturnal and wander around their habitat taking any suitable prey that they stumble into. If this happens to be a nest of baby birds, a roosting small bird, a small mammal or a small reptile, rather than an insect, then so be it. If the spider is big enough to handle the prey then it will kill it and feed on it.

The Araneomorphae (True Spiders)

With many more families and vastly more species, the true spiders have a much greater range of prey catching methods than the mygalomorphs, though there are some parallels between them. The family Segestriidae, the tunnel or sixeyed spiders, represented in North America by just a handful of species, build a silken tube in cracks in rocks, under bark or stones or, in Europe at least, in crevices in buildings. From this tube a fan of silk triplines runs across the surface, which function just as those described above.

In parallel with the free living bird-eating spiders are the short-sighted hunters, mainly nocturnal, who wander around and blunder into and catch any suitable size prey. These include a specialist found on both sides of the Atlantic, *Dysdera crocata*. Called the woodlouse (sowbug) spider in the UK, it lives beneath stones or other objects, most often around human habitations, where sowbugs are numerous. It has huge fangs enabling it to pierce the armor plating of its prey. The same fangs can give a painful bite to humans if the spider is handled carelessly, though its poison is harmless.

Not all of the short-sighted hunters are nocturnal with one family, the crab spiders mainly day active. They are very much sit-and-wait predators. Typical is the common flower or goldenrod spider, *Misumena vatia*, widespread in both North America and Europe. The female, who is white with red marking on the abdomen, is very noticeable, at least to us, as she normally sits in the center of a flower. She poses, with her front two pairs of legs held out in front of her as if she is about to hug something, which indeed she is. Should some hapless insect, often a bee or hover fly, come too close, she wraps her legs around it and delivers a fast-acting, fatal bite.

The family Pisauridae, which includes the fishing spiders, the Ctenidae, or wandering spiders, the Oxyopidae, lynx spiders, and the Lycosidae, wolf spiders, have fairly large front eyes, especially the latter family, and they hunt more actively than the short-sighted hunters. They still spend a lot of the time sitting and waiting but the rest of the time they

A number of crab spider species typically sit in flowers
and capture insects visiting to collect nectar and pollen. This female is
feeding on a fly that was quickly dispatched by her potent poison.

Certain species of Pisauridae can run on the surface of water and catch
insects that have fallen in. They also have the ability to reach below the surface to
catch tiny fish or tadpoles, giving them the common name of fishing spiders.

wander from place to place, presumably increasing the likelihood of coming across suitable prey. Sun-loving wolf spiders, for example, will sit on the ground, apparently basking for a while, and then suddenly rush off to another site, where again they will sit for a while before repeating the action. Similar activity can be observed in the lynx spiders but more often on vegetation than on the ground. Some members of the genus *Dolomedes*, the fishing spiders, hunt on the surface of lakes and ponds. The name fishing spider is not strictly accurate, for their main prey is insects which have fallen into the water and cause ripples by thrashing about on the surface. Normally the spider, sitting with its front feet in contact with the water surface, detects the ripples and rushes over to subdue the prey. On occasions, however, they have been seen to snatch small fish and tadpoles from just below the water surface.

Perhaps the only true hunters amongst spiders are the jumpers, for the majority of them actively search out prey rather than waiting for it to come along. Surely the best species to study in this group is the zebra spider, *Salticus scenicus*. The zebra spider is widespread on both sides of the Atlantic and comes with the advantage that it lives on the outside of human habitations, occasionally straying indoors. With its black carapace and zebra striped abdomen it is easily recognized as it scurries around in our homes, stopping now and again to sweep the surrounding area with its large forward-pointing main eyes, in search of prey. It will even look directly at the observer, as if weighing up whether this might be a very large meal. Hold out a finger and often as not it will jump on to it. As the spider does so, a silken safety line attached to its previous perch runs out behind it, so if the spider misses the target, it will only fall a short distance before hauling itself back up. The lucky observer might see it catch sight of small prey, when it seems to sit back on its heels before launching itself on to the unlucky insect. Although having nowhere near the jumping ability of a grasshopper or a flea, some jumping spiders are capable of leaping around fourteen times their own body length.

The Web Builders

When it comes to the web-builders the immediate image that comes to mind is that of the orb web. This is perhaps the most sophisticated of all webs and is used by members of three families, the Uloboridae (hackled orbweavers), Tetragnathidae (longjawed orbweavers), and Aranaeidae (the orbweavers). The largest orb webs known are made by members of the genus *Nephila* and can exceed 6ft (nearly 2m) across. The orb web is used to catch flying insects and in its straightforward form is represented by that of the garden spider, *Araneus diadematus* and its relations. In these spiders the web is normally placed vertically but in other spiders it may be horizontal or placed at an angle. A number of these orbweavers, including *Argiope* and *Cyclosa* species, incorporate a structure called a stabilimentum into the center of their web. This consists of zig-zags of white silk, arranged in a cross or in spirals in the center of the web (see page 44). There has been much discussion as to its role. A recent piece of published research indicating that it attracts bees does not really ring true, as these particular spiders, at least in the worldwide context, do not often encounter bees, and their favorite prey seems to be jumping orthoptera such as grasshoppers.

Beyond this, all sorts of modifications occur, some of which are quite interesting. The ladder web spider, *Scoloderus cordatus*, an orbweaver from Florida is an extreme example, taking as long as three hours to build its web. At the base is the normal, vertically placed orb web but from the upper edge the spider builds a mesh ladder, the width of the orb web and sometimes more than 3ft (1m) long. This web is specialized for catching moths. When one of these flies into a normal orb web its scales stick to the sticky silk and effectively gum it up, allowing the struggling moth to shake free. A moth colliding with the ladder, on the other hand, shakes itself free only to slip down the ladder onto further sticky silk until eventually it no longer has enough scales to save it and it becomes trapped.

While *Scoloderus* spends a great deal of time building its web another araneid, *Wixia ectypa*, does the opposite. Its web consists of a simple set of non-sticky radial threads,

A golden orb-web spider, Nephila madagascariensis, *sits at the centre of her web in Madagascar. The spirals of yellow silk are covered in hundreds of sticky droplets which trap any prey flying into the web.*

strung between a couple of twigs on a bush, which the spider remains in contact with. An insect walking along the twig will alert the spider, which then rushes over to subdue it. Unlike normal orb web spiders, which wrap the prey by spinning it round and round in the web, *Wixia* runs round and round it on the twig as it covers it in silk.

The alternative to using the whole orb web is to use a part of it and this is the case with the triangle spiders of the hackled orbweaver family, which has species in both North America and Europe. They make a triangular web with only four radii, roughly one sixth the area of a complete orb. The spider sits at what would be the center of the web holding the triangular section taught with its legs. If an insect flies into the sticky triangle the spider immediately loosens its grip and the silk collapses, surrounding the prey. The spider is now in a position to immobilize it by wrapping it with a swathe of silk.

A common house spider, Tegenaria domestica, *on her web.*

The ultimate in orb web reduction is to end up with just a single strand. It may seem a strange development, to have evolved a complicated and effective structure like the orb web only to then discard it in its entirety, but single strand spiders seem just as effective as those with a complete web. *Miagrammopes simus*, a hackled orbweaver spider from tropical America, perches on a single, horizontal, non-sticky line. She sits on this line and lowers a length of very sticky thread below her, into which small insects fly and are trapped. *Phoroncidia studo* uses even less silk than *Miagrammopes*, just a single, sticky horizontal line.

She sits at one end of this and waits until several tiny male sciarid flies become trapped on it. The spider then lets out silk behind her, and rolls up the silk in front of her until she has the mass of flies in her jaws. These tiny flies seem to pay more attention to the web than might normally be expected and it is postulated that the spider coats it with some chemical attractant, perhaps similar to that secreted by female flies of the species.

Chemical mimicry is almost certainly used by those most interesting of creatures, the bolas spiders in the Araneidae family. These are represented in North America by *Mastophora bisaccata*, from Florida, Texas and the Gulf States, though from personal experience it is either not very common or it is very difficult to find. This spider hangs on a single line and dangles a short length of silk from one of its legs, on the end of which is a blob consisting of a mass of sticky silk. This contains chemicals which mimic those of the female of certain moths, and the males are thus attracted to it. As a male moth approaches the spider whirls the sticky blob rapidly round and round until it touches and catches the insect. The spider then reels the moth in. The author was lucky enough to observe a female *M. bisaccata* on a visit to Florida. The moth catching action was so fast that, even though he was watching the spider, found that the prey was on the end of the spider's line in the blink of an eye.

Apart from the orb webs there are two other types which are commonly encountered. A number of different spiders live in a silken tube which opens out onto a flat, dense sheet of silk. In both North America and Europe one is likely to encounter such a structure in the corners of sheds, barns or garages. These are the webs of the house spiders of the genus *Tegenaria*. An insect falling onto or walking onto the sheet immediately attracts the attentions of the resident spider, who rushes out across the sheet to dispatch it. Out in the country the grass spiders, *Agelena* in Europe and *Agelenopsis* in North America build sheet webs in grass and low vegetation. These spiders have triplines above the main sheet making it more difficult for an insect to escape before the spider descends on it. Cobweb weaver spiders produce an untidy looking scaffold structure containing a mixture of non-sticky and sticky threads. Insects flying into this rather untidy mess of silk blunder around trying to escape but inevitably get caught. A combination of sheet and scaffold is constructed by the sheetweb, or 'gossamer' spiders. The sheet, below which the spider hangs, is often domed and above it is a complex of scaffold lines. Insects

A net-casting spider is poised to drop its web and capture prey.

collide with the scaffold lines, fall onto the sheet and the spider rushes over and bites it through the silk. It then pulls the prey through the web and wraps it, returning later to repair the hole in the sheet.

Cribellate spiders, with their hackled band silk, produce untidy webs, relying upon walking prey to become entangled in the fluffy threads. One family has, however, given up a fixed web but instead they hold it in their legs and throw it over the prey. These are the ogrefaced or 'net-casting' spiders with one species found in Florida. The net, which is very elastic, is formed by the hind 3 pairs of legs, while the spider hangs from the front pair. She then turns round, picks the web up in the front two pairs of legs and holds it stretched out before her. Some species hang close to the ground and drop the net over walking insects as they pass by, others hang higher up and drop the net over flying insects. If the prey is trapped successfully, the elastic net contracts and is wrapped around it. The spider then bites the prey through the silk and commences to feed.

A mass of dew-covered dwarf weaver webs in damp grassland.

Spider Defenses

Although all spiders are predators they themselves end up as prey to many other animals. As a result spiders have a number of ploys which reduce the likelihood that they will end up as a meal. Enemies come in a number of forms: birds, lizards, bats, frogs and toads, and hunting and parasitic wasps to name but a few. As might be expected, defenses against one kind of enemy are not necessarily of use against another.

The vertebrate predators actively seek out their prey and the best defense against this is either to hide or appear to be something inedible. One way of hiding, at least from the birds and wasps, is to be active at night only and this is true of many spiders. The alternative is to have a lair in which to hide, emerging only to catch prey. Living in a burrow, as many tarantulas and wolf spiders do, is one way of achieving this. Many web-dwelling spiders have a silken lair somewhere on or near the web in which they remain until they rush out to grab a meal. Some orbweavers remain motionless at the center of the web but for one particular predator this is no defense. The world's largest damselfly, which lives in Costa Rica, specializes in pulling these spiders off the middle of their web and devouring them.

Many spiders are cryptic or camouflaged, i.e., they have a coloration which blends in with the surroundings in which they live. Spiders that live on bark are good examples. They can be very difficult to spot unless they move, which could prove fatal if a predator is in the vicinity.

Another form of defense is 'protective resemblance', in the past referred to as mimicry. In this case the spider resembles something in its surroundings which a vertebrate predator, such as a bird or lizard, would not bother to investigate. So there are spiders that mimic leaves, sticks, flowers, buds and bird-droppings. Spiders from a number of different families resemble ants. Ants are usually avoided by visually hunting predators, such as birds, as ants

Lichen spiders are difficult to spot against the tree trunks on which they live.

often have an unpleasant sting, are quite tough, have powerful jaws, do not taste particularly nice and may produce unpleasant chemical sprays. Not only do some spiders mimic ants in their looks but many also mimic their behavior. How do they do this since ants have six legs and antennae and spiders have eight legs and no antennae? The answer is quite simple, the spiders walk along on their six hind legs and wave the front pair of legs around, mimicking the ant's antennae. Some of these spiders are so good at mimicking the ants that they live amongst that they are able to walk up to them, kill and feed on them with no response from the other ants. Interestingly, there is some experimental evidence to show that looking like an ant protects spiders from another visual predator, the hunting wasp. The contents of mud-dauber wasp nests, which are supplied with paralyzed spiders on which the wasp larvae feed, was examined in an area of central Africa. The nests contained spiders from many families, but the only species missing were the two common ant-mimics from the local area. Certain salticid and clubionid spiders resemble another unpleasant insect, the female mutillid wasp. These insects have a very unpleasant sting and are avoided by most potential predators so resembling one should pay off for a spider.

There are ways in which spiders actively defend themselves when in danger. Many species, both free-living and web dwellers, will drop to the ground on a safety line when threatened. Some web dwellers can violently shake their web to make it difficult for an enemy to get a fix on them. Many of the tarantulas (Theraphosidae) from the Americas raise their abdomen when attacked and if the aggressor does not retreat, the spider shakes a cloud of irritating hairs into its face. The world's largest spider, *Theraphosa leblondi,* warns off enemies by hissing, a bit like a snake, by rubbing together some modified hairs on its legs. Large tarantulas, such as the western desert tarantula, will rear up on their hind legs and present their fangs when cornered. The well-known and poisonous funnelweb and Brazilian wandering spiders are particularly dangerous because they are actually prepared to attack and bite an opponent.

Perhaps the greatest enemies of spiders are the spider-hunting wasps. Even
though spiders are predators, the female wasps are able to approach and sting them,
inducing paralysis, before dragging the spiders back to their burrows as food for their larvae.

Spiders and Man

It is an undoubted fact that spiders are either tolerated or despised by most people, with only a few who actually like them. Spiders are very useful in that their main prey is insects, many of which are pests, so for that reason alone most of us tolerate them. Surveys show that fear of spiders is greater in females than in males, though of course the latter are much less likely to admit to such a fear. Such fears may be passed from generation to generation. In the author's family, for example, his daughters' dislike comes from the reactions of their mother towards spiders. There are, however, people whose hate or fear of spiders is so great that it becomes an illness, known as arachnophobia. In extreme cases such folks will not enter a room unless it has been thoroughly searched and cleared of any spiders present.

Fear of spiders in the United Kingdom makes no great sense, since there are no species harmful to humans. There are, however, around 25 species worldwide that are venomous to man. In North America there are a number of quite dangerous species, especially in the southern and western states, while Australia and several countries in South America also have highly venomous species. In reality just how dangerous are these spiders? In the USA the widow spiders, *Latrodectus* species, pose the greatest threat to humans, in that they can in extremely rare instances cause death. Not for more than 20 years, however, has anyone in the USA definitely died as a result of a bite from a black widow, mainly because of the excellent health care available to victims and the ability in extreme cases of envenomation, to administer an antitoxin, or antivenom. The likelihood of being bitten by one is in fact fairly low, for they are very retiring spiders and hide at the earliest opportunity when disturbed. They are only likely to bite a human if they are accidentally pressed against the skin in some way. The other unpleasant North American

The black widow's bite is unpleasant, but only dangerous to the very young and very old.

spider is the brown recluse, *Loxosceles reclusa*. Whereas the widows inject a venom which upsets the nervous system, the brown recluse injects a tissue-digesting venom. This can cause serious ulceration at the bite site unless it is treated early. A hole large enough to take a tennis ball was reported to the author as having been caused by a brown recluse bite.

Elsewhere, Australia has its own dangerous widow spider, *Latrodectus hasselti*, there called the redback, whose venom has similar effects to those of the American species. Figures indicate that roughly 2000 people are bitten each year by the redback. A recent study revealed that of 56 genuine redback attacks only two thirds were serious and just six people required the use of an antivenom. The other highly venomous spiders in Australia are the funnelwebs, mainly *Atrax robustus*, the Sydney funnelweb but also *Hadronyche* species, all mygalomorphs. In particular it is the males, wandering around in search of the sedentary females, who cause most bites, for they will attack without provocation when cornered. Unusually for spiders it has been found that male venom is several times more toxic than that of females. As with widow spiders, deaths from funnelweb bites are very rare, just 13 between 1927 and 1980 when an antivenom was introduced.

In South America, and in particular Brazil, live the wandering spiders of the genus *Phoneutria*, said by some to produce the most toxic venoms of any spider. Whether this is true or not these spiders can cause death, though once again these are very few. During the 70 years up to 1996 just 14 deaths were recorded in Brazil, one every five years and in more recent studies, only seven percent of people bitten required the application of the now widely available antivenom.

A wandering spider in the Ugandan rainforest. Some related Brazilian wandering spiders are among the most dangerous to man, and can attack with their highly toxic poison.

Glossary of Biological Terms

Araneomorphae – the so-called true spiders with jaws that bite towards one another in a pincer - like action.

calamistrum – a row of curved spines on the hind legs of cribellate spiders used to comb out and fluff up hackled-band silk.

cephalothorax – the combined head and thorax of spiders.

chelicerae – spider jaws consisting of a basal segment with a fang hinged on it.

cribellum – a flat plate with numerous spigots that produce hackled-band silk.

epigyne – a special female structure which matches the male palp during mating and helps to prevent cross-fertilization between species.

Mygalomorphae – more primitive spiders with forward pointing jaws which bite downwards onto the prey.

pedipalps – more often written as 'palps', these are appendages on either side of the mouth associated with taste. The terminal segment is used as a mating structure in male spiders.

pheromones – chemical messengers, usually airborne but may be waterborne or attached to silk.

rastellum – a set of large teeth on the jaws of trapdoor spiders used in burrow digging.

spermathecae – sacs in female spiders used to store semen obtained from males during mating.

spigots – tiny nozzles through which silk is emitted from the spinnerets.

stabilimentum – a pattern of thickened silk, often a zig-zag cross, found at the center of the web of certain araneid spiders.

trichobothria – hairs on the legs of spiders sensitive to air movement and vibrations.

Recommended Reading & Useful Websites

The Book of the Spider by Paul Hillyard (Hutchinson, London, 1994) delves into all aspects of spiders and also their relationships to us humans.

The American Arachnological Society website at www.americanarachnology.org/index.html is an extremely good place to start as a source of information on spiders and their relatives.

Another comprehensive website, with links to hundreds of others relating to spiders is The Arachnology Home Page at: http://www.arachnology.be.

The Australian Museum online has an interesting section on spiders at: http://www.amonline.net.au/spiders/.

Biographical Note

Rod Preston-Mafham is an accomplished writer and photographer in the world of natural history. He was educated in zoology and agriculture in London, and is a founding partner of the leading wildlife photographic agency Premaphotos. He has worked as a biology teacher and is the author or co-author of over twenty books on nature. When not observing spiders, he enjoys his interest in steam locomotives.

Common Spider Families

Families marked **RED** contain some venomous species which can be a harmful to humans.

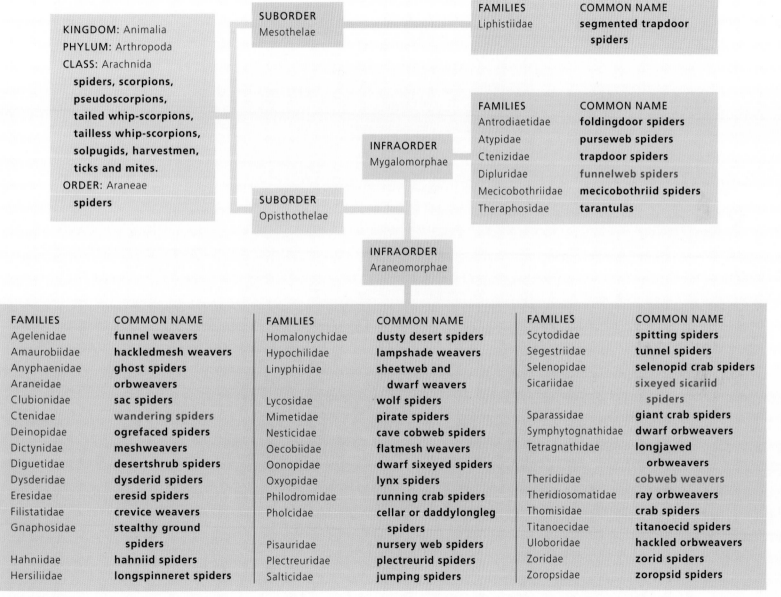

KINGDOM: Animalia
PHYLUM: Arthropoda
CLASS: Arachnida
   spiders, scorpions,
   pseudoscorpions,
   tailed whip-scorpions,
   tailless whip-scorpions,
   solpugids, harvestmen,
   ticks and mites.
ORDER: Araneae
   spiders

SUBORDER Mesothelae

SUBORDER Opisthothelae

INFRAORDER Mygalomorphae

INFRAORDER Araneomorphae

FAMILIES	COMMON NAME
Liphistiidae	**segmented trapdoor spiders**

FAMILIES	COMMON NAME
Antrodiaetidae	**foldingdoor spiders**
Atypidae	**purseweb spiders**
Ctenizidae	**trapdoor spiders**
Dipluridae	funnelweb spiders
Mecicobothriidae	**mecicobothriid spiders**
Theraphosidae	**tarantulas**

FAMILIES	COMMON NAME	FAMILIES	COMMON NAME	FAMILIES	COMMON NAME
Agelenidae	**funnel weavers**	Homalonychidae	**dusty desert spiders**	Scytodidae	**spitting spiders**
Amaurobiidae	**hackledmesh weavers**	Hypochilidae	**lampshade weavers**	Segestriidae	**tunnel spiders**
Anyphaenidae	**ghost spiders**	Linyphiidae	**sheetweb and**	Selenopidae	**selenopid crab spiders**
Araneidae	**orbweavers**		**dwarf weavers**	Sicariidae	sixeyed sicariid
Clubionidae	**sac spiders**	Lycosidae	**wolf spiders**		spiders
Ctenidae	wandering spiders	Mimetidae	**pirate spiders**	Sparassidae	**giant crab spiders**
Deinopidae	**ogrefaced spiders**	Nesticidae	**cave cobweb spiders**	Symphytognathidae	**dwarf orbweavers**
Dictynidae	**meshweavers**	Oecobiidae	**flatmesh weavers**	Tetragnathidae	**longjawed**
Diguetidae	**desertshrub spiders**	Oonopidae	**dwarf sixeyed spiders**		**orbweavers**
Dysderidae	**dysderid spiders**	Oxyopidae	**lynx spiders**	Theridiidae	cobweb weavers
Eresidae	**eresid spiders**	Philodromidae	**running crab spiders**	Theridiosomatidae	**ray orbweavers**
Filistatidae	**crevice weavers**	Pholcidae	**cellar or daddylongleg**	Thomisidae	**crab spiders**
Gnaphosidae	**stealthy ground**		**spiders**	Titanoecidae	**titanoecid spiders**
	spiders	Pisauridae	**nursery web spiders**	Uloboridae	**hackled orbweavers**
Hahniidae	**hahniid spiders**	Plectreuridae	**plectreurid spiders**	Zoridae	**zorid spiders**
Hersiliidae	**longspinneret spiders**	Salticidae	**jumping spiders**	Zoropsidae	**zoropsid spiders**

Abridged from:
Breene, R.G. (ed.). 2003. Common Names of Arachnids, 5th edition. American Arachnological Society, online at: http://www.americanarachnology.org/AAS_information.html

Index

*Entries in **bold** indicate pictures*